HOO   Hood, Susan.
ER
           Look! I can read!

$13.89

DATE			

Put Beginning Readers on the Right Track with
ALL ABOARD READING™

The All Aboard Reading series is especially for beginning readers. Written by noted authors and illustrated in full color, these are books that children really and truly *want* to read—books to excite their imagination, tickle their funny bone, expand their interests, and support their feelings. With four different reading levels, All Aboard Reading lets you choose which books are most appropriate for your children and their growing abilities.

Picture Readers—for Ages 3 to 6
Picture Readers have super-simple texts, with many nouns appearing as rebus pictures. At the end of each book are 24 flash cards—on one side is the rebus picture; on the other side is the written-out word.

Level 1—for Preschool through First-Grade Children
Level 1 books have very few lines per page, very large type, easy words, lots of repetition, and pictures with visual "cues" to help children figure out the words on the page.

Level 2—for First-Grade to Third-Grade Children
Level 2 books are printed in slightly smaller type than Level 1 books. The stories are more complex, but there is still lots of repetition in the text, and many pictures. The sentences are quite simple and are broken up into short lines to make reading easier.

Level 3—for Second-Grade through Third-Grade Children
Level 3 books have considerably longer texts, harder words, and more complicated sentences.

All Aboard for happy reading!

For Emily—S.H.

For Mark, who sometimes reads to me—A.W.

Text copyright © 2000 by Susan Hood. Illustrations copyright © 2000 by Amy Wummer.
All rights reserved. Published by Grosset & Dunlap, a division of Penguin Putnam Books
for Young Readers, New York. ALL ABOARD READING is a trademark of The Putnam &
Grosset Group. GROSSET & DUNLAP is a trademark of Grosset & Dunlap, Inc. Published
simultaneously in Canada. Printed in the U.S.A.

Library of Congress Cataloging-in-Publication Data is available.

ISBN 0-448-42282-4 (GB)   A B C D E F G H I J
ISBN 0-448-41967-X (pbk.) A B C D E F G H I J

ALL
ABOARD
READING™
Level 1
Preschool-Grade 1

Look! I Can Read!

By Susan Hood
Illustrated by Amy Wummer

Grosset & Dunlap • New York

I can read "Milk."

I can read "Stop."

I can read "School."

I can read
"Shop."

I know my letters
from A to Z.

A is for ant.

B is for bee.

What starts with C?
Carrots and cheese.

Can you find something here

for each one of these?

Look at the picture and find an object
that begins with each letter from D to Z.

I wrote my name.

I'll read it to you.

Mommy, can <u>you</u> read this?

See? I love you!

My dad reads to me
at bedtime each night.

He shows me you read
from the left to the right.

milk ✓
pizza
coffee
apples ✓
bananas

Now I read words
in the grocery store.

I can read words

in a tree...

...on the floor.

The pictures help me
as I read and I look.

Hey, Mommy,
guess what!

I read this
whole book!